IMAGES
of America

MONROE AND
WEST MONROE
LOUISIANA

AERIAL VIEW OF WEST MONROE, 1957. This view of West Monroe features the Lea Joyner Bridge across the Ouachita River. The Old Union Oil Mill is the complex of buildings near the bridge. These buildings have been demolished and will someday have condominiums take their places. Coming from Monroe, the first street to the left is Antique Alley, a popular shopping area. (Courtesy Ouachita Parish Public Library Special Collections Archives.)

IMAGES
of America

MONROE AND WEST MONROE
LOUISIANA

Ouachita Parish Historical Interest Group

ARCADIA
PUBLISHING

Published by Arcadia Publishing
Charleston, South Carolina

Library of Congress Catalog Card Number: 2002103043

For all general information contact Arcadia Publishing at:
Telephone 843-853-2070
Fax 843-853-0044
E-Mail sales@arcadiapublishing.com
For customer service and orders:
Toll-Free 1-888-313-2665

Visit us on the Internet at www.arcadiapublishing.com

For Robert "Bob" Tirmenstein, a singular man and wonderful friend, and for Lucia.
Bob left us with many happy memories.

BAYOU DESIARD. Picturesque Bayou Desiard was named for an early French trapper. Desiard lived in a cottage on the bayou and named it for himself. When Don Juan Filhiol came to the area he kept the name. (Courtesy Ouachita Parish Public Library Special Collections Archives.)

CONTENTS

Acknowledgments   6

Introduction   7

1. People and Families   9

2. Schools, Churches, and Synagogues   33

3. Local Scenes   53

4. Homes and Lodging   67

5. Fun and Games   77

6. Local Businesses   97

7. Floods   113

ACKNOWLEDGMENTS

When I agreed to accept the responsibility of putting together a pictorial history of Monroe and West Monroe, I immediately began to make calls to enlist the help of those who I knew to be much more knowledgeable about the history of the "Twin Cities" than myself. Almost everyone I approached agreed to help. Should I fail to mention the name of anyone who helped, please forgive the oversight and know that I thought of adding them to the list as soon as the book was ready to be printed. My apologies in advance for any omissions.

Thanks and acknowledgements go to the following: Dr. Russ Williams, for sharing his knowledge, and for the loan of some of the photos from his collection; the staff of the Ouachita Parish Public Library Genealogy Department for assistance in research and in typing (and for their good natures); Patricia Gilman, Lora Peppers, Mary Roberson, and Lucia Tirmenstein; Nan Gorton, Ron Downing, Rachael S. Ober, Jewel Rogers, Roseanne Marx, Jean Mintz, and Sandra Blate for many ideas and photos from Temple B'Nai Israel Archives. All of these people made valuable contributions with ideas, photos, identifications, and organization. Many thanks also to Katie White of Arcadia for her unlimited patience.

—Ann Middleton

INTRODUCTION

This unique recollection of Monroe, Louisiana was found in a drawer of the Ouachita Parish Library in the office of the former operations coordinator Shirley Montfort. The author is unknown and it has been printed as it was written.

Come follow me down Desiard Street in 1951 and see what you remember. Going from the old bridge (they call it the Endom Bridge now) to the east. On the south side of the street is Western Union. The best job a teenage boy could hope to have. Next was New South Drug, where I worked for a while until Arthur Mathews took my place (Are you listening?), then Monroe Blueprinting. The Tom McCann, where everyone got their back-to-school shoes. Next, Ouachita National Bank, where you could get on the elevator and the operator would say "Floor please." (Unless it was Fred, and me and then he would just tell us to use the stairs.) Across the street on the corner was D. Masur & Son, where all the rich people bought their clothes. Then there was a door that opened to some stairs. I don't remember what was up there. Then on the corner, Kelso's Children's Shop. On the next corner, the Style Shop, where Jerry Richards worked part time. He got killed some years ago in an auto accident. Moving on down was the Hemp's Cafeteria. Joy and I never went in there. Then the Capitol Theater where I saw Cyrano de Bergerac with my main squeeze and held her hand. The the Vogue Shop. And then the infamous WALGREEN DRUG STORE! Where if you stood on the corner on any Saturday you would see everyone you knew. (I also sold papers on this corner.) Across Desiard were Peacock's Jewelry and the Palace Dept. Store. Then Lerners next to Franks Shoe Store, where Joe Milner and I sold shoes on Saturdays. Then, on the corner, Leggits Drug. Across Desiard, on the corner was Butlers Shoe Store, where Fred and Glen Fleming sold shoes on Sat. Next, Holloway & Thompson Shoe Store, where I got my first job after Joy and I got married. Then The Toggery mens store next to the three 5&10 stores, Kress, Woolworth and Morgan and Lindsey. Across Desiard was Central Bank, still there, [2002] Remember the big clock? Then Fields shoe store. (Where all the teenage girls bought their shoes.) As I remember, and I get a little hazy here, on down the street was Sears, Silversteins, Dew Music and Bell Pharmacy, where you could buy an ice cream cone and read all the funny books you wanted to. (Did any of you ever swap funny books?) Across the street on the corner was the Paramount Theater, the only place in Monroe that was air-conditioned.* I remember how we used to stand in front of the door to feel the cool air until the white haired lady came out and ran us off. Ah, and the midnight shows. Going down the street was R & A jewelry, Kraus and Kahn, the Buckhorn pool hall, and Primos Café, which had the best chocolate pie in town. Across the street, Peoples Homestead, R.C. Brown, the Upstairs Poolhall, which Fred and I frequented, and the Joy Theater, where you could see the same movies that were playing at the Paramount for half as much. A year later, I can still hear my mother telling me to wait till it comes to the Joy. Then there was Elias & Son, and Hunt & Whitaker. Across the street Shorty Guiterrez sold hot tamales on the corner out of his pushcart. I still get them made by his daughter. The Circle S Service Station was on the corner. Then Kellers bicycle shop, Coney Island (Still eat their hot dogs, too), a domino parlor, the Alvis hotel restaurant, Melody Bar (Drank many a beer here listening to Fred Dunn play the piano and sing) and on the corner the Alvis Hotel. That brings us to the 500 block, and the only things I remember are the Shamrock Bar on the corner and the Log Cabin on the next corner with the Majestic Hotel over the Log Cabin. Billy Mancusos parents managed the Majestic Hotel. By the way, the Shamarock [sic] is still open and going strong. [At the time of this writing, 2002] Amazing what endures in this world! Is this a message?

Let's wander around on some of the side streets now. The 100 block of South Grand was known as the "Gold Coast." There was Sam's Bar, and on down the Brown Derby. Going on down you go by the Monroe Hotel, where Ed Miller earned the title "The Nude Dude." I'm not going into exactly how. Next was the courthouse and on down the hallowed halls of learning, OPHS. There's no reason to go any further, except for a few establishments I might mention: Across the street was my favorite hangout, Faulks. Then the choir house and on down Tichelis Gro. Where you could buy 3 cigarettes for a nickel.

The next street east was St. John. Going down it was the Virginia Hotel, then the city hall (Hate that that building was torn down). Then the fire station. And the courthouse and Wright Bendel Clinic with a pharmacy in the basement. Across from the city hall was the First Baptist Church. With the health unit on the corner.

Next over was Jackson St. where streetcars ran at one time, but not in 1951. (This is for you, Billy and Theresa.) Going down Jackson, we pass the infamous Frances Hotel. Then St. Mathews [sic] Catholic Church. Probably one of the prettiest buildings in Monroe today. Next is the post office, now known as the federal building, where I started and ended my career in the postal service. Next was the First Methodist Church, where Mary Bays Serex's father was minister. Across the street was the St. Frances [sic] Hospital. Remember the fishpond in the front? Across the street was Central Grammar School. Remember the turrets? On south across the street was B'Nai Israel Jewish synagogue. Another beautiful building lost. Next, Anna Meyer Library, the only library in Monroe. Now we have three, but I think I enjoyed the days at Anna Meyer the most.Now we've come to Catalpa Street. On the east is Johnson Bros. Barber Shop. And the Monroe rec. where Jimmy Vaughn wasted many a Saturday trying in vain to find true love. On the west side of the street; Kornmans Meat Mkt., Parker's Jwlr., A&P Gro., The Sugar Bowl. (Where I didn't get my butt kicked.) Then Bonds Bakery, the best chocolate éclairs in the world. The next corner, H. Mickel, and the First Presbyterian Church. Another beautiful building gone.

I know I have left out some things and put some in places they never were, but, then, you wouldn't have anything to try and remember.

*Another prominent local remembers the huge dill pickles at the Paramount, where African-Americans were required to sit upstairs.

Many thanks to the author of this reminiscent history. But, in turning the pages of this pictorial volume, we hope that additional fond memories will be awakened. Recall the professional baseball teams, the Natatorium, the lovely old homes that once stood on South Grand and Jackson Streets, when "Five Points" was not today's "Five Points." Indeed, "come follow me" through the pages of time as we journey back to Monroe and West Monroe's celebrated past.

One

PEOPLE AND FAMILIES

ANDREW A. FORSYTHE AND SARAH JANE FORSYTHE. Andrew and Sarah were the children of Capt. James Forsythe and Narcissa White Forsythe. Andrew A. Forsythe became a doctor and later mayor of Monroe. (Courtesy Ouachita Parish Public Library Special Collections Archives.)

LUCIA AND BOB TIRMENSTEIN. Lucia Lewis and Robert Tirmenstein were married February 1, 1953, in First Baptist Church of Monroe, Louisiana. Lucia was the daughter of Assia Lewis and Nettie Powe Lewis Moore, while Robert was the son of Robert Leo and Louise Elmore Tirmenstein. (Courtesy Ouachita Parish Public Library Special Collections Archives.)

MISS FRANCES FLANDERS, LIBRARIAN. An extremely progressive librarian, Miss Flanders worked for the Ouachita Parish Public Library for 27 years. (Courtesy Ouachita Parish Public Library Special Collections.)

MAYOR FORSYTHE. Mayor Andrew A. Forsythe's body laid in state at Monroe City Hall in 1914. (Courtesy Ouachita Parish Public Library Special Collections Archives.)

MR. ERNEST NEVILLE. Ernest Neville was one of 15 children. He came to Monroe in 1901 to serve as assistant principal to the Monroe city schools, and was made superintendent of all the schools in 1910. Neville High School, erected in 1931, was named for him. Besides being known as one of the best public educators in the state, he was also Monroe's beloved educator and a friend to children. (Courtesy Ouachita Parish Public Library Special Collections Archives.)

MR. AND MRS. THOMAS WASHINGTON MENYWEATHER. Thomas Washington Manyweather and his wife Francis were both born into slavery in Ouachita Parish. In 1871, they homesteaded 80 acres of land on the west bank of the Ouachita River. In 1881, they farmed an additional 40 acres adjacent to their original plot. Steamboats were busily plying up and down the river transporting products to and from Monroe. The Manyweather place was one of the sites where docks were situated to load and unload goods. The family still has possession of almost all of the land as well as the original documents concerning the property. Admiral and James Manyweather are grandsons of Thomas Washington Manyweather and Mrs. Mary Roberson is a great-granddaughter. (Courtesy Ouachita Parish Public Library Special Collections Archives.)

REV. WARNER WASHINGTON HILL JR.
Reverend Hill was born to slave parents in Gilbert, Louisiana, in 1870. He learned his ABCs in Sunday school. He always struggled to further his education, so he studied at night while working on the railroad during the day. He climbed the ladder to become the first president of the Louisiana Home and Foreign Mission Baptist State Convention Inc. He was a national church leader, a great organizer, thinker, and minister during his nearly 40-year ministerial career. His son, Dr. S.D. Hill, became one of the first highly respected African-American medical doctors in the Monroe community. Dr. Hill's clinic at 2001 Grammont Street in Monroe is named for him. (Courtesy Mrs. Jacqueline Simmons.)

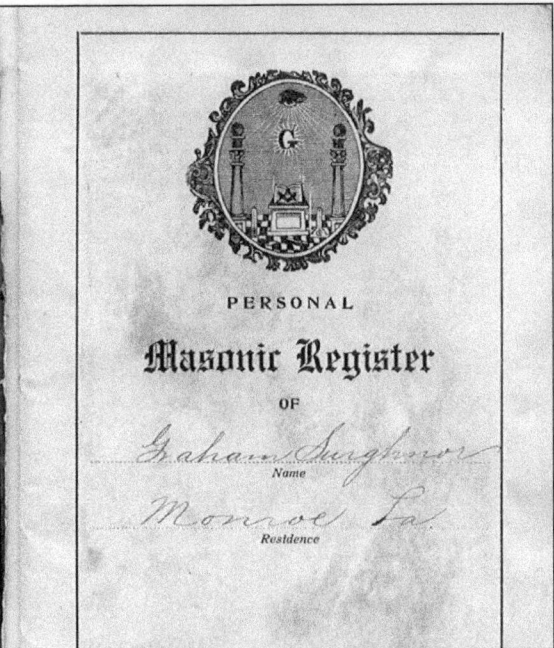

DR. GRAHAM SURGHNOR. Dr. Surghnor was an eye, ear, nose, and throat doctor whose office was located on the second floor of Allen's Pharmacy. (Courtesy Ouachita Parish Public Library Special Collections Archives.)

RICHARD BARRINGTON. Mr. Barrington helped establish the first school for blacks in Monroe. He was a former slave of Solomon Weathersbee Downs. After numerous frustrating attempts to set the school in motion, his efforts ultimately resulted in Carroll High School in the 1950s. The story of Richard Barrington's life is interesting and exciting, not only for his overcoming the adversities of his life, but for his kindness toward many of those who caused him problems. (Courtesy Dr. E. Russ Williams.)

JAMES A. NOE SR. Noe was the owner of KNOE-TV and radio stations; he is pictured here with Huey P. Long. (Courtesy Ouachita Parish Public Library Special Collections Archives.)

LAWRENCE GIBBS. Mr. Gibbs is originally from Monroe, Louisiana. He was a Louisiana State Senator, locally known as the "Old Left-Hander." He appeared on KMLB and KNOE television, in addition to emceeing a radio lunch program called "Dining at St. Francis [Hotel]. (Courtesy Dr. E. Russ Williams.)

MR. W.J. MILLS. Mr. W.J. Mills was the owner of Braswell & Mills Mercantile Store on Trenton Street in West Monroe, Louisiana. He was a successful businessman and a member of the Knights of Pythias Lodge in Monroe. The photo was taken in March 1943. (Courtesy Frankie Mills.)

W.J. MILLS GROCERY STORE, MONROE, LOUISIANA. The grocery store still stands on the banks of the Ouachita River. (Courtesy Frankie Mills.)

W.J. MILLS GROCERY STORE, MONROE, LOUISIANA. Probably taken c. 1912, this photo of W.J. Mills Grocery Store shows Octave B. Register on the far left. (Courtesy Frankie Mills.)

BRASWELL & MILLS GENERAL MERCHANDISE. George Mills is shown in the doorway of the mercantile store of Braswell & Mills on Trenton Street in West Monroe. (Courtesy of Frankie Mills.)

GEORGE LEE JR. Lee was photographed at the age of two or three in 1922 or 1923. He later became a teacher at Ransom School, where he taught from 1955 to 1963. (Courtesy Frankie Mills.)

LOYCE MILLS. Loyce told the photographer that her doll "had broken an arm and was going to die." (Courtesy Frankie Mills.)

JORGA BARKHAM GEORGE. Shown here with her doll and buggy, Jorga was the daughter of Lula Houston Barkham. The family resided in West Monroe, Louisiana. (Courtesy Frankie Mills.)

MILLS FAMILY. From left to right are George Lee, R.V. Mills, and daughter Loyce, *c.* 1922. The little boy is George Lee Jr., who later became the photo owner's husband. (Courtesy Frankie Mills.)

LULA HOUSTON BARKHAM. Lula Houston Barkham and her sister R.V. Houston Mills are seen pictured in this *c.* 1896 photograph. (Courtesy Frankie Mills.)

(*above, left*) MARY ELIZA MILLS, C. **1890**. Mary "Mollie" Eliza Mills was a member of the W.J. Mills family. (Courtesy Frankie Mills.)

(*above, right*) JENNIE MILLS. Jennie, *c.* 1898, was the daughter of Jerry Mills. She died at an early age of a fever. (Courtesy Frankie Mills.)

(*below, left*) MILLS FAMILY. Pictured in this December 25, 1900 photograph, from left to right, are George Lee Mills Sr., Ernest Mills, and Willie Jerry Mills. (Courtesy Frankie Mills.)

(*above, left*) **GEORGE LEE MILLS SR.** This photo of George Lee Mills Sr. was taken *c.* 1900. Mr. Mills was born in 1848 and died in 1922. (Courtesy Frankie Mills.)

(*above, right*) **GEORGE LEE MILLS SR.** A slightly older George Lee Mills is seen here. He was the father-in-law of Frankie Mills. (Courtesy Frankie Mills.)

(*below, right*) **MRS. BARKHAM.** Mrs. Barkham had a hat shop in West Monroe. She moved to Texas in 1917 to open a hat shop there as well. (Courtesy Frankie Mills.)

STRIKING A POSE. Pictured *c.* 1917, Lula Houston Barkham probably designed the hat herself. (Courtesy Frankie Mills.)

MISS BELLE MILLS. Born in 1879, Belle Mills is seen here around 1899. She attended seminary school in Louisville, Kentucky, and Fort Worth, Texas (the Baptist Theological Seminary). She taught music for a time in Fort Worth. Mills lived in Monroe and West Monroe most of her life and was a charter member of the First Baptist Church of West Monroe. (Courtesy Frankie Mills.)

BELLE MILLS, 1914. William C.
Church, who bought out E.W. Mealy
when he retired, took this photo of
Miss Belle Mills. The photography
shop was located at 116 South Grand
Street. (Courtesy Frankie Mills.)

A-1 STANDARD SCHOOL. Miss Belle Mills
posed with a proud Sunday school class
in 1918. She is shown here on the steps
of the West Monroe First Baptist Church,
second row, fifth from left. (Courtesy
Frankie Mills.)

LOUISIANA FIRST BAPTIST CHURCH. First Baptist Church Monroe Sunday school class posed for a picture in 1918. Miss Belle Mills is on the second row, far right. (Courtesy Ouachita Parish Public Library Special Collections Archives.)

THE WELCOME. The male members of the W.E. Mills family of West Monroe are seen on *The Welcome* (except for the little girl posing at the rear of the boat). (Courtesy Frankie Mills.)

Form No. 1.—Oath to be Taken by Those Who Were Never Disfranchised.

UNITED STATES OF AMERICA.

State of Louisiana—Parish of Jackson.

Oct 19½ 1868.

I C.W. Mills do solemnly swear, or affirm that I am twenty-one years of age, was *born naturalized* in the United States, and am subject to the jurisdiction thereof, and have been a resident of the State of Louisiana since the 1 22 day of Oct 1867 , and a resident of this Parish since the 1 22 day of April 1858 , and that I am not disfranchised for any of the causes stated in the first paragraph of Article Ninety-nine of the Constitution of this State.

And I do further solemnly swear, or affirm, that I did not hold any office, civil or military, for one year or more, under the organization styled "the Confederate States of America;" that I never registered myself as an enemy of the United States; that I never acted as leader of guerrilla bands during the late rebellion; that I never, in the advocacy of treason, wrote or published newspaper articles, or preached sermons, during the late rebellion; that I never voted for and signed an ordinance of secession in any State.

C.W. Mills

Sworn to and subscribed before me this Oct 1868.

C.W. MILLS'S "OATH TO BE TAKEN BY THOSE WHO WERE NEVER DISFRANCHISED." In other words, he swore to have never been connected, in any way, with the Confederate States of America.

DR. E.D. SMITH. Dr. Elizabeth D. Irby Crow Smith (1832–1905) was a longtime resident of Cadeville, Ouachita Parish, Louisiana, with extended family throughout Ouachita and neighboring parishes. She was one of the first female doctors in North Louisiana. She was descended from a long line of physicians, and made house calls in a covered buggy pulled by a large red horse named Frank. A wicker basket held some of her medical supplies. (Courtesy Colleen Grant Hardin.)

DR. OLIVER BROWN SMITH. Dr. Oliver Brown Smith, seen here, was Elizabeth Irby Smith's second husband. (Courtesy Colleen Grant Hardin.)

MEDICAL FORMULAS. These formulas for medicines were made and used by Dr. Elizabeth Irby Smith in her practice. The ingredients listed here are "two pints of alcohol, a 1/2 pint of ammonia, 1 gallon of castor oil, oil of bergamot (enough to perfume)—give four drops for congestive fever. Gelseminum fluidrachims; tincture of aconite, 24 drops. Dose 30 drops. Where there is much pain in stomach, nausea, vomiting. Extract of stramonium, one gram; sulphate of morphine, one gram; sulphate of quinine, eight grams—Rub well together and divide into four doses." (Courtesy Colleen Grant Hardin.)

HEADACHE RECEIPT. This is a "headache receipt from Dr. D.A. Johnson" to Dr. Elizabeth Irby Smith. (Courtesy Colleen Grant Hardin.)

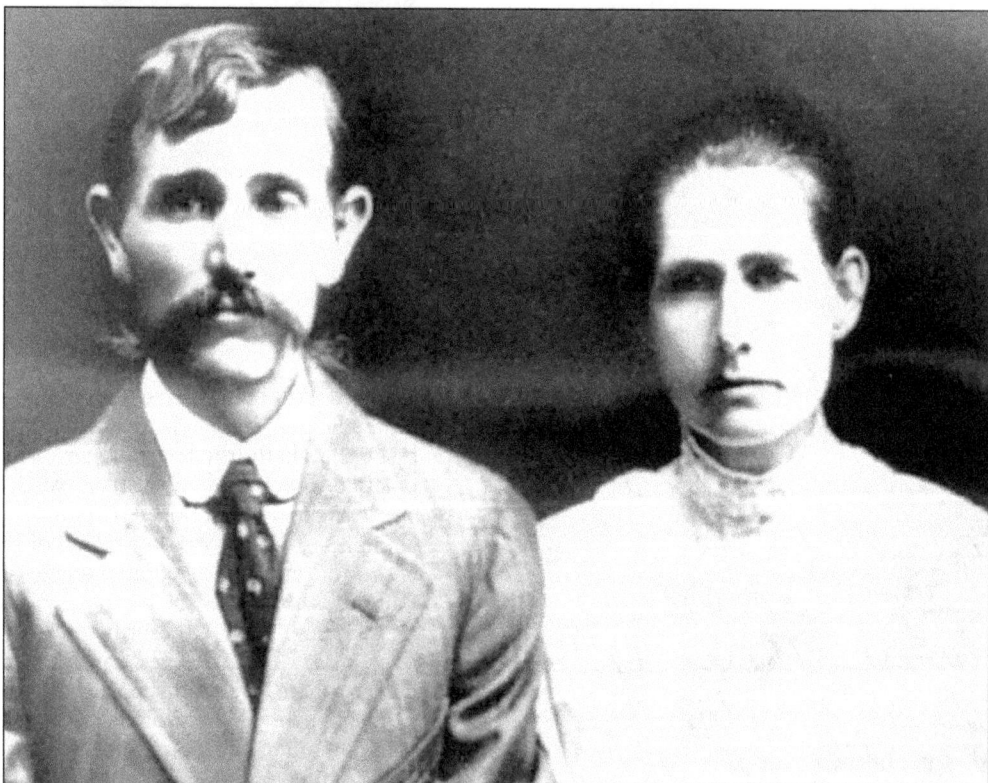

MR. AND MRS. REUBEN HENRY GRANT. Reuben Henry Grant and his wife, Emma Florence Smith Grant, daughter of Dr. Elizabeth Irby Smith, are pictured above. (Courtesy Colleen Grant Hardin.)

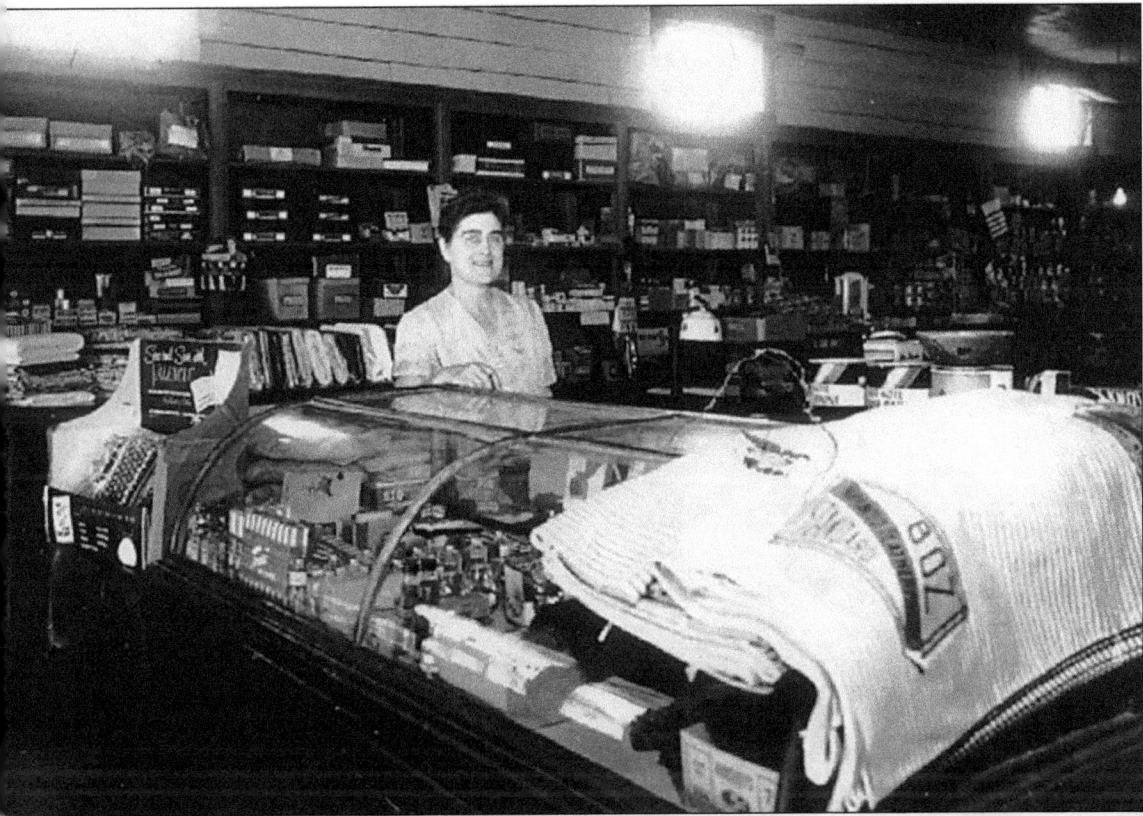

LEILA FLORENCE GRANT TOUSLEY HARPER. Leila was the daughter of Emma and Reuben Henry Grant and granddaughter of Dr. Elizabeth Irby Smith. She is pictured in the R.H. Grant Store, Eros, Louisiana. Eros is located just across the western border of Ouachita Parish in Jackson Parish. (Courtesy Colleen Grant Hardin.)

RED CROSS GREY LADIES. The Red Cross Grey Ladies are seen here during World War II.

(Courtesy Temple B'Nai Israel Archives.)

PHOTO OP. The photo above includes Monroe Mayor and Mrs. Ralph Troy, President Ronald Reagan, a Monroe city police officer, and a secret service agent in 1982 at Monroe Municipal Airport. (Courtesy Dr. E. Russ Williams.)

PRESIDENT RONALD REAGAN. The President and Mayor Ralph Troy are seen speaking to members of Northeast Louisiana University Band in 1982. (Courtesy Dr. E. Russ Williams.)

Two

SCHOOLS, CHURCHES, AND SYNAGOGUES

OLD BOSCO SCHOOL. According to the caption on the back of this photograph, "This was the old Bosco School many years ago before Bosco experienced its population explosion." The old building also served as a Baptist church well into the 20th century. (Courtesy Ouachita Parish Public Library Special Collections Archives.)

CONFIRMATION CLASS, TEMPLE B'NAI ISRAEL, JUNE 4, 1919. These young people are, from left to right, (front row) Irwin Shlemker, Mildred Levy (Mrs. Seymour Solomon), Roselynn Lieber (Mrs. Clifford M. Strauss), Alan Sugar, and Mathilde Goldman; (back row) Dr. David, Emile Kaliski, Rosalia (Bobbie) Kaliski (Mrs. William Goldsmith), Dorothy Callman, Patricia (Pat) Kaplan (Mrs. Alan Sugar Sr.), Herman Marks, and Carolyn Cahn (Dr. Leon ?). (Courtesy Temple B'Nai Israel Archives.)

JACKSON STREET. Taken after 1906, this view shows the first Temple B'Nai Israel with the rabbi's house on an adjoining lot in the extreme left of the photo. (Courtesy Frankie Mills.)

OLD JEWISH SYNAGOGUE. Although this building is often referred to as the "Old Jewish Synagogue," its predecessor, also located on Jackson Street is called Temple Sinai in the *Monroe Evening News, World's Fair Issue* of 1893. It was reported in the paper that "Here in Monroe the Jewish Church is in a very prosperous condition. Their synagogue Temple Sinai is a beautiful brick building, elegantly furnished, with a commodious parsonage, located on an adjoining lot. The church membership consists of 40 families, about 150 souls." The building shown here, before its demolition, stood where St. Francis Hospital parking garage is today. (Courtesy Temple B'Nai Israel Archives.)

TEMPLE SINAI SYNAGOGUE. This synagogue at 115 Jackson Street was referred to in the 1912–1913 Monroe City Directory as "Sinai Temple Congregation, B'Nai Israel." The rabbi at that time was Rabbi Israel Heinberg. (Courtesy Temple B'Nai Israel Archives.)

MONROE, LOUISIANA FIRST BAPTIST CHURCH LEADERS. Only two of the church leaders could be identified. Among the church's leaders are C.E. Bynum (first row, second on the right) and Dr. M.E. Weaver, fifth pastor of the church in 1928 (second row, first on the left). (Courtesy Ouachita Parish Public Library Special Collections Archives.)

GOSPEL CHOIR. This photo of the gospel choir was taken from the Centennial-Dedication and Program of Ground Breaking Service. (Courtesy Mrs. Ollie Burns.)

PRESBYTERIAN CHURCH, C. 1911. The First Presbyterian Church of Monroe was located at the corner of Grammont and Catalpa Streets. (Courtesy Ouachita Parish Public Library Special

MONROE, La.

Collections Archives.)

39

KEAL'S CHORUS

Row 1—Armentha Henderson, Jacqueline Washington, Shelia Pollard, Cloteal Lee, Michael Flintroy, Helen Smith.
Row 2—Gregory Benjamin, Sybil Thomas, Sandra Pollard, Rita Allen
Row 3—Ardell Hamilton, Mattie Berry
Row 4—Ricky Brown, Wanda Clark, Bonita Richards
Row 5—Dexter Morrison, Linda Henderson, Dinah Henderson
Row 6—Herbert Brice, Percy Brown, Calvin Henderson, Wilford Flintroy

CHERUBIM CHOIR

Row 1—Pearl Wilson, Donald Richards, Wendell Bonner, Jacqueline Benjamin, Wanda Richards, Harolyn Hammonds, Nency Johnson, Thomas Benjamin, Reginald Kelson
Row 2—Robert E. Johnson, Debra Benjamin, Monica Pierce, Michelle Pierce
Row 3—Linda Richards, Curley Richards, Sharon Henderson, Michael Brown, Melvin Johnson, Donald Wade.
Row 4—Carrie Vonner, Karla Wade, Betty Henderson.

JUNIOR USHERS

Row 1—Lorraine Perkins, Robert Johnson, Ronald Brown, Michael Brown, Michelle Pierce, Linda Richards, Evelyn Brice
Row 2—Wendill Bonner, Reginald Kelson, Harolyn Hammonds, Curley Richards, Debra Benjamin, Melvin Johnson
Row 3—Monica Pierce, Sharon Henderson, Donald Wade
Row 4—Karla Wade, Betty Henderson, Shirley Stringfellow, Alma Stringfellow
Row 5—Ronald Perkins, Donald Richards, Ricky Brown

KEAL'S CHORUS, CHERUBIM CHOIR, AND JUNIOR USHERS. (Courtesy Mrs. Ollie Burns.)

BOARD OF DEACONS AND TRUSTEES. These photos are from the programme of the Ground-Breaking Service of First Baptist Church, Swayze Street, Monroe, Louisiana, August 9, 1970. (Centennial-Dedication of New First Baptist Church, Courtesy Mrs. Ollie Burns.)

41

ST. PASCHAL'S CHURCH, 1941. St. Paschal's Church was founded in 1940. As it is the primary aim of every parish to provide a thoroughly Catholic education for its children, on May 5, 1941, groundbreaking ceremonies were held for St. Paschal's School. Rev. Henry Freiburg, O.F.M. was the church's first pastor. By 1958 St. Paschal's had a new school. A new church was completed in 1964 on North Seventh Street in West Monroe. The photo shows St. Paschal's first confirmation class. (Courtesy Ouachita Parish Public Library Special Collections Archives.)

St. Paschal's Church, 1942. On January 19, 1941, the church was formally dedicated and blessed by His Excellency Bishop Desmond. Daily Mass began the next day. By 1967 the church had grown from the group shown above to 500 families and has, of course, grown even more by 2002. (Courtesy Ouachita Parish Public Library Special Collections Archives.)

MONROE CITY HIGH SCHOOL STUDENTS, 1913. Mr. Ernest Neville (front row, 11th from left) is among the Monroe City High School students of 1913 pictured above. (Courtesy Ouachita Parish Public Library Special Collections Archives.)

MONROE CITY HIGH SCHOOL, 1907. The graduating class of 1907 included, from left to right, (top row) Abe Kaplan, Lynnton Ethridge, and Mary Johnston; (bottom row) Rosa Marx, Iris Newton, Lillian Masengill, and Barkdull Faulk. In 1888 the first four graduates of the Monroe City School System had completed the requirements for graduation—all four were women. (Courtesy Temple B'Nai Israel Archives.)

44

CITY HIGH SCHOOL. The programme for the laying of the cornerstone of City High School is pictured to the right and below. (Courtesy Dr. E. Russ Williams.)

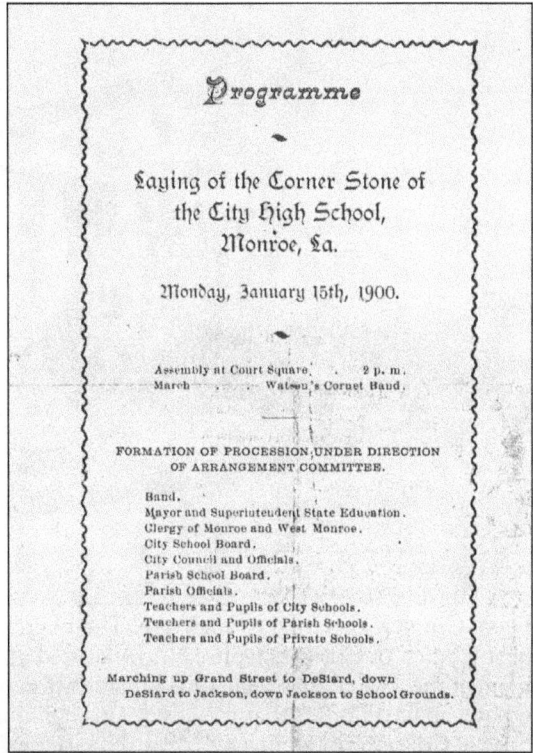

Programme

Laying of the Corner Stone of the City High School, Monroe, La.

Monday, January 15th, 1900.

Assembly at Court Square, 2 p. m.
March Watson's Cornet Band.

FORMATION OF PROCESSION UNDER DIRECTION OF ARRANGEMENT COMMITTEE.

Band.
Mayor and Superintendent State Education.
Clergy of Monroe and West Monroe.
City School Board.
City Council and Officials.
Parish School Board.
Parish Officials.
Teachers and Pupils of City Schools.
Teachers and Pupils of Parish Schools.
Teachers and Pupils of Private Schools.

Marching up Grand Street to DeSiard, down DeSiard to Jackson, down Jackson to School Grounds.

Committee of Arrangement.

A. A. FORSYTHE, Mayor.

C. A. DOWNEY, Chairman School Board.

I. HEINBERG, Secretary School Board.

W. B. REILY, Councilman.

B. J. SUGAR. Councilman.

Order of Ceremony.

1. Music by Watson's Cornet Band.
2. Mayor's Address.
3. Music.
4. Laying of Corner Stone by Hon. J. V. Calhoun State Superintendent of Education.
5. Dedication Ode. Chorus.
6. Short Addresses.
7. "America," Chorus by Children.

COMMITTEE OF ARRANGEMENT. When the cornerstone for Monroe City High School was laid on January 15th, 1900, the ceremonies began with music by Watson's Cornet band. (Courtesy Dr. E. Russ Williams.)

FIRST CHURCH OF CHRIST SCIENTIST. The church was first located on Auburn Avenue. The First Church of Christ Scientist is now located at 970 Filhiol Avenue. There is also a reading room at the Twin Cities Mall. One library patron recalls a lovely, cream-colored ginger jar with ornate, applied flowers that was inside this building. (Courtesy Ouachita Parish Public Library Special Collections Archives.)

NEVILLE HIGH SCHOOL AROUND 1939. On 20 acres of land across from the municipal golf links and swimming pool, Neville High School opened its doors to 559 students in 1931. Of those, 190 were junior high students and 369 were in grades 9 through 12. (Courtesy Ouachita Parish Public Library Special Collections Archives.)

MONROE CITY HIGH SCHOOL, LATER CENTRAL GRAMMAR SCHOOL. Names listed on the back of the picture include Eita Johnson, Mary Etta Chase, Leonora Lieber, Nancy Dushay, Lily Williams, Alma ?, Roslyn Renaud, Molly Fleaming, Casel Apgar, Gertrude Dautrive, Sallie Humble, and Olive Gunby. The site is now Anna Gray Noe, across from St. Francis Hospital. (Courtesy Ouachita Parish Public Library Special Collections Archives.)

NEVILLE BAND MARCHES TOWARD THE WHITE HOUSE

NEVILLE BAND MARCHES TOWARD THE WHITE HOUSE. Neville High School Marching Band of Monroe, Louisiana, was featured in the inaugural parade for Pres. John F. Kennedy on Jan. 20,1961. The citizens of Monroe contributed funds for three buses and expenses, making it possible for the students to participate. (Courtesy Ouachita Parish Public Library Special Collections Archives.)

COLORED HIGH

COLORED HIGH SCHOOL. Monroe Colored High School was completed in 1923 on Breard Street. It is the current site of the J.S. Clark Magnet School. It was vacated in 1952 and replaced by Carroll High School, which is presently located on Renwick Street in Monroe. The first Ouachita Colored School was organized in 1867 and had as its leaders Anthony Overton, Sandy Bird, Perry Jackson, George Green, Duncan Hill, John Small, and Emanuel Thorton. (Courtesy Dr. E. Russ Williams.)

SENIOR CLASS MEMBERS. Some of the members of the Carroll High School senior class of 1956 are to the right. These photos appeared in the 1956 Carroll High School yearbook *BullDog*. (Courtesy Mary Roberson.)

LYNETTA MARINOAUX WILLIS
Choir, Majorette, Library Club, Modernique Club.

JANETTE P. HOSTON
Annual Staff, Digest Staff, Basketball, Science Club.

FLORENCE ANITA TAYLOR
Majorette, Concert Band, Science Club.

JESSIE MAE FELTON
Band, Science Club.

KALISKI BRANTLEY
Choir, Science Club.

WILEY THOMPSON
Dramatics, Science Club.

FELIX DECATUR
Football, Baseball.

CAROLYN LOUDD
Choir, Mordernique Cl

WALTER BRISCO
Football, Basketball.

THOMAS HOLMAN

THIRD GRADE CLASS. This third grade class is featured in Monroe High School's 1957 yearbook *BullDog*. While the students are unidentified, their teacher was noted as Mr. H.L. McClanahan. (Courtesy Mary Roberson.)

THIRD GRADE

FOURTH GRADE

FOURTH GRADE CLASS. This fourth grade class photograph was featured in Monroe High School's 1957 yearbook *BullDog*. (Courtesy Mary Roberson.)

MONROE COLORED HIGH SCHOOL 1928 GRADUATES. The old Monroe Colored High School provided one of the few opportunities for blacks to learn how to read and write. Built in 1923 on the present site of Clark Elementary School, the high school's enrollment was nearly 700 students. It was vacated in 1952 and replaced by Carroll High School presently located on Renwick Street. In 2002, four of the students in the first graduating class (pictured here) still lived in the same Monroe neighborhood. (Courtesy Mary Roberson.)

PLAYGROUND AT GRAMMAR SCHOOL. The playground of Booker T. Washington Grammar School was photographed *c.* 1951. (Courtesy Ouachita Parish Public Library Special Collections Archives.)

Some of the Courses Offered
by the
Ouachita Parish Public Library
1000 Stubbs Avenue
Monroe, Louisiana 71201

Ouachita Parish Junior College

Monroe, Louisiana

1931-1932 School Year

Any person of good moral character who can meet the college entrance requirements (graduate of a standard high school or equivalent) may enter the Ouachita Parish Junior College.

Only first year courses will be offered this session. Below are listed suggested first year curricula from which the student should choose one.

ARTS AND SCIENCE

Required:

English	6 hours
Physical Education	2 hours

Elect 24 hours from the following:

Health and Hygiene	Psychology
Chemistry	European History
Biology	Political Science
French	College Algebra
Latin	Trigonometry
Spanish	

INTERMEDIATE OR LOWER ELEMENTARY
TEACHER'S COURSE

English	6 hours
Biology	8 hours
Psychology	6 hours
History or Mathematics	6 hours
Physical Education	2 hours
Literature for the Grades	4 hours
Health and Hygiene	4 hours

ENGINEERING

English	6 hours
Chemistry	8 hours
European History	6 hours
Mathematics	6 hours
Mechanical Drawing	6 hours
Physical Education	2 hours

PRE-MEDICAL

English	6 hours
Foreign Language	8 hours
Mathematics	6 hours
Biology	8 hours
Chemistry	8 hours
Physical Education	2 hours

PRE-LEGAL

English	6 hours
History	6 hours
Political Science	6 hours
Foreign Language	8 hours
Mathematics	6 hours
Physical Education	2 hours
Elective	2-4 hours

AERIAL VIEW OF NORTHEAST JUNIOR COLLEGE, C. 1950S. T.O. Brown, superintendent of the Ouachita Parish Schools, outlined his plan for a junior college in Monroe at a Kiwanis Club luncheon in the fall of 1927. In 1928 the state legislature established Ouachita Parish Junior College. The University of Louisiana at Monroe grew from this junior college, which opened its doors on September 28, 1931. (Courtesy Ouachita Parish Public Library Special Collections Archives.)

Three

LOCAL SCENES

MONROE CIVIC CENTER. The Monroe Civic Center opened September 1, 1967. The building includes a 2,250-seat theater, 7,200-seat arena, and a multi-purpose conference hall. The cost of the building was $5.5 million. (Courtesy Dr. E. Russ Williams.)

CITY BUILDINGS AND BRIDGES. Pictured from left to right, top to bottom, are the following: Left aisle, City Market; Vicksburg, Shreveport and Pacific Railroad Bridge; City Market; Right Aisle, City Market; Foot and Wagon Bridge over Ouachita River between Monroe and West Monroe; and City Power House. (Courtesy Ouachita Parish Public Library Special Collections Archives.)

ST. JOHN STREET. LOOKING NORTH. MONROE. LA

ST. JOHN STREET. On the left side of the street are city hall, the police station, the Virginia Hotel, and the Ouachita Bank Building. On the right side of the street sits First Baptist Church, the post office, the Castle Hall building (which was once Standard Office Supply c. 1930s), and the Bernhardt Building. (Courtesy Ouachita Parish Public Library Special Collections Archives.)

MONROE, LA.   Pine St.

PINE STREET, AFTER 1906. The first building on the left would later become Mrs. Cook's boarding house at Pine and North Second Streets, Monroe, Louisiana. (Courtesy Ouachita Parish Public Library Special Collections Archives.)

DESIARD STREET LOOKING EAST. This view showcases the Capital Theater, the Buckhorn Bar and Saloon next door to the theater, Krogmire Tailor Shop, The Woman's Shop, and the Ouachita National Bank on the right. (Courtesy Temple B'Nai Israel Archives.)

223–225 Desiard Street, c. 1930s. The photographers at Griffin Studios took this photo. Note the trolley tracks. The Palais Royal was listed in the 1930 Monroe City Directory, so the date is approximated. (Courtesy Ouachita Parish Public Library Special Collections Archives.)

Paramount Theatre. The Saenger Theatre Chain of New Orleans bought the Sugar Theatre Building located at 301 Desiard Street. It was built in 1912 by Barney, Sam, and Isadore Sugar as an upstairs theatre with stores and shops on the ground floor. (Courtesy Howard Jackson.)

CITY OF MONROE. Taken c. 1951, this view of Monroe was included in a brochure that was submitted to Assistant Secretary of the Air Force, Hon. Harold C. Stuart. The purpose of the brochure was to reactivate Selman Field to further the defense program of the United States. (Courtesy Dr. E. Russ Williams.)

MUNICIPAL BUS SYSTEM. Pictured here are three of the twenty-six municipal buses of 1951. (Courtesy of Ouachita Parish Public Library Special Collections Archives.)

DESIARD STREET BUSINESSES. On the left side of Desiard Street, c. 1960, was Silverstein's, an exclusive ladies apparel shop, owned and operated by David Silverstein. Sam Rubin and Will Abramson founded R&A Jewelers, a fine jewelry shop specializing in estate jewelry. R&A is still in business on Desiard Street as of this printing. They celebrated 75 years in business in 2002. Sam Rubin Jr. now owns the store. Jack and Nan Dew owned Dew Music Co., which specialized in band instruments, pianos, and stereo equipment. Kraus & Cahn was a gentleman's clothing store started by Louis Krauss. Stuart and Bobbie Doenberg owned and operated the store in the 1960s. The Paramount Theater was originally the Saenger Theater. It featured vaudeville shows, plays, and later movies. Such greats as Jack Benny, Al Jolson, and W.C. Fields entertained there. (Courtesy Ouachita Parish Public Library Special Collections Archives.)

DESIARD STREET, C. 1970s. The empty building shown here was occupied for a while by the Shamrock Bar. Frances Towers can be seen in the background. (Courtesy Ouachita Parish Public Library Special Collections Archives.)

SELMAN FIELD THEATRE, C. 1951. The side of the building reads "Back the Attack. Buy More Bonds." Selman Feild also had two chapels, both located near this theatre, a swimming pool, four athletic fields, and an advanced cadet recreation room. The base also had a football squad and a basketball squad. By 1956 this building had been demolished. (Courtesy Ouachita Parish Public Library Special Collections Archives.)

SELMAN FIELD SWIMMING POOL. This photo from 1951 shows the swimming pool with barbed wire around it. (Courtesy Ouachita Parish Public Library Special Collections Archives.)

OLD MONROE CITY MARKET. Originally located at 400 Desiard Street (corner Catalpa Street), the market was composed of only two aisles—right and left aisles. The market was owned by the City of Monroe. (Courtesy Ouachita Parish Public Library Special Collections Archives.)

BAYOU DESIARD COUNTRY CLUB. This photo was taken right after the country club was chartered in June of 1945. The club boasts an eighteen-hole golf course, five dining rooms, lighted tennis courts, and a swimming pool. (Courtesy Ouachita Parish Public Library Special Collections Archives.)

E.A. CONWAY MEMORIAL HOSPITAL. In March of 1994, the old E.A. Conway Memorial Hospital was to be set aside for use as a youth drug treatment center. It was abandoned in 1987 when a new hospital was built. From 1987 to 2002, the building has sat vacant because asbestos must be removed before it can be used again. Construction of the hospital was completed in 1939, and on July 1, 1941, Charity Hospital of Monroe (its first name) opened its doors. (Courtesy Ouachita Parish Public Library Special Collections Archives.)

FEDERAL BUILDING ON JACKSON STREET. This *c.*1933 Works Projects Administration photo highlights the Federal Building. (Courtesy Ouachita Parish Public Library Special Collections Archives.)

Issued by Monroe & Shreveport Stage Line.

MINDEN, LA.,
To St. Louis.

EXCHANGE TICKET.

Good for one First Class Passage
FROM MINDEN, LA.,
To Destination Written Above.
Upon the following Conditions, viz:

This Coupon will not be received for passage
on Trains, but must be exchanged at the Ticket
Office of the North Louisiana and Texas Railroad,
at Monroe, for a through Ticket, Baggage Checked
through from Monroe to Destination.

FORM EX. 3.

NOTE.—Ticket Agent of the N. L. &
T. R. R. will enter below the Form,
Number and Date of Issue of Ticket
for which this Coupon is exchanged.

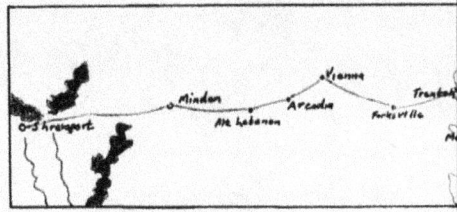

Issued by Monroe & Shreveport Stage Line.

MINDEN, LA.,
To New Orleans.

EXCHANGE TICKET.

Good for one First Class Passage
FROM MINDEN, LA.,
To Destination Written Above.
the following Conditions, viz:

NOTE.—Ticket Agent of the N. L. &
R. R. will enter below the Form,
and Date of Issue of Ticket
which this Coupon is exchanged.

This interesting stage line operating between Monroe & Shreveport was named just that by the headings of the stage tickets here shown.

A. C.C. Chaffe and Jas. F. McGuire seemed to be the principal owners, and operators. The main office was in Minden, La.

As can be seen the stops tied in with the North Louisiana & Texas Railroad Co. of Monroe in handling passengers and freight.

In leaving Monroe it took about two days of travel with time out only for sleeping to get to Shreveport over this old stage line.

MINDEN, LOUISIANA. This interesting stage line operating between Monroe and Shreveport was named just that by the headings of the stage tickets shown. In leaving Monroe it took about two days of travel with time out only for sleeping to get to Shreveport over this old stage line. (Courtesy *Louisiana: Its Street and Interurban Railways*, by Louis C. Hennick, Journal Printing Co.: Shreveport, Louisiana, 1962.)

PARISH COURT HOUSE. MONROE, LA.

OLD COURTHOUSE. The small building in the front of the Old Courthouse is the old bandstand. Concerts and political rallies were held there. This courthouse building was torn down and today's courthouse is now on this site. A note on the back of the postcard reads "You are cordially invited to visit Monroe, Louisiana, May 4-6, 1911, and attend the Louisiana Farm Land Congress. Bring your bathingsuit and enjoy a swim in the 'Radio-Salt Water Natatorium' now open to the public free." (Courtesy Ouachita Parish Public Library Special Collections Archives.)

EAST AND WEST DESIARD STREET. Headed east is Louisville Avenue. Headed north is Old Sterlington Highway. Tower Texaco and Tower Grill can be seen approximately center of the photo on Louisville. On the corner of Desiard is Slagle Johnson Lumber Company. (Courtesy Ouachita Parish Public Library Special Collections.)

FRANCES HOTEL, NOW FRANCES TOWERS, 1986. The Frances Hotel first opened its doors in 1931. It was the "in" place for social gatherings. The hotel's entire top floor served as a ballroom. It was named for Frances McEnery, wife of the founder of Delta Airlines. In 1978, it was converted to senior citizen housing with 130 apartments. In the 1950s, a lighted beacon atop the Frances Hotel served as a landmark for travelers. The light shone 40 to 60 miles away. (Courtesy Ouachita Parish Public Library Special Collections Archives.)

MONROE, LA.   Marketing Hay.

MARKETING HAY, MONROE, LOUISIANA. New South Drug Store, Ltd. in Monroe had this real postcard photo published in Germany. (Courtesy Ouachita Parish Public Library Special Collections Archives.)

Four

HOMES AND LODGING

HAPPY HOME, ROLAND ROAD, MONROE, LOUISIANA. The silos are now gone from this location. (Courtesy Dr. E. Russ Williams.)

RIVERSIDE SANITARIUM. Originally constructed at 3001 South Grand Street, the Riverside Sanitarium building no longer stands. After its use as a hospital it became Riverside Convalescent Home and was later demolished. Dr. A.D. Tisdale Sr. owned and operated the hospital from 1934 until his death in 1935. Rev. Frank Tripp, a former pastor of the Monroe First Baptist Church, founded the institution. (Courtesy Ouachita Parish Public Library Special Collections Archives.)

SIG HAAS RESIDENCE, C. 1905. In 1912 Sig Haas was president of Monroe Building and Loan association and vice-president of Monroe Realty and Immigration Association, Ltd. His home, shown here, was at Louisville Avenue, at the corner of Front Street. (Courtesy Temple B'Nai Israel Archives.)

805 WALNUT STREET. Ernest Fudickar's home is pictured above. Fudickar, a native of Germany, immigrated to the United States in 1880. He embarked on a career as a retail grocer and joined the firm of N.P. Cook and Co. He was a member of the Monroe City Council in the 1900s. (Courtesy Ouachita Parish Public Library Special Collections.)

LAYTON CASTLE. In 1814, Henry Bry, originally from Switzerland, acquired some riverfront property in Monroe. He built a cottage and named it Mulberry Grove because he wanted to promote a silkworm industry in Louisiana. The outbuilding today known as the wine cellar was the original building for housing the silkworms (the industry did not take off). Approximately 60 years later, an addition was added to the original cottage by outdoor staircases. Then, in the early 1900s, Mrs. Robert Layton III remodeled the house after one she had seen in France. This lovely home at 1112 Jackson Street holds many fascinating memories and tales of a ghost. (Courtesy Ouachita Parish Public Library Special Collections.)

THE CASTLE, A.H. BERNHARDT'S RESIDENCE. This house was located on North Third Street.
(Courtesy Ouachita Parish Public Library Special Collections Archives.)

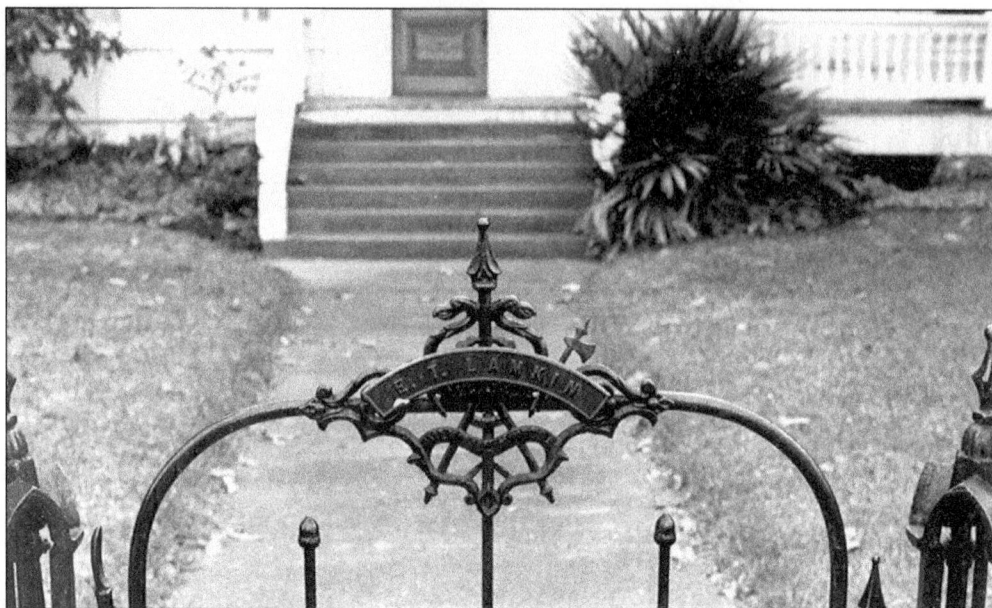

BRIGHT-LAMKIN-EASTERLING HOME. This lovely home, built in 1890, still maintains its Victorian grandeur at 918 Jackson Street in Monroe. In 1986, it was added to the National Register of Historic Places. (Courtesy Ouachita Parish Public Library Special Collections Archives.)

OUTSIDE VIEW OF BRIGHT-LAMKIN-EASTERLING HOME. This is the best example of Queen Anne architecture in Ouachita Parish. The house has statewide significance because of its painted slate mantles. (Ouachita Parish Public Library Special Collections Archives.)

HOTEL VIRGINIA. The Hotel Virginia was located on St. John and Grammon Streets; today it is the site of the State Office Building. The hotel opened its doors on November 15 (or 16), 1925, at a cost of $75,000. The local newspaper, *The Monroe News-Star*, described the six-storied building as "having a large and accommodating roof garden surmounting the upper floor and when in summer this will be adorned with potted flowers." The setting was the site for many dinner dances as well as countless high school proms. The columned building was Monroe Building and Loan Association. Adjacent to the columned building was the former Ouachita National Bank. The exclusive Lotus Club was housed on the tenth floor of the bank building. (Courtesy Ouachita Parish Public Library Special Collections Archives.)

MONROE HOTEL

Chas. L. Bradley, Manager.

MONROE HOTEL. Advertised as "the leading hotel from 1900 to 1929," the hotel had 250 rooms and was nine stories high. This hotel served Sunday dinner for 75¢, which included the following: chicken gumbo, saltwater trout, roast chicken and dressing, sweetbreads, and a variety of vegetables and beverages. The merchant's lunch was 25¢ and included a choice of three meats, vegetables, soup, and a beverage. (Courtesy Ouachita Parish Public Library Special Collections Archives.)

HOTEL ALVIS. This c. 1950s photo of the hotel was probably taken during its heyday. (Courtesy Dr. E. Russ Williams.)

ALVIS HOTEL LOBBY. Built by Fred Kalil in 1928, the Alvis Hotel was referred to in its heyday as "the working man's Waldorf Astoria." Legend has it that part of the concrete and steel building was built over quicksand, and that 300 bales of cotton were used to fill in the hole. Even in the 1950s, a single room with a tile shower was only $3.50 per night. It was sold in 1969 and renamed the Barron Hotel. However, Kalil reacquired it two or three years later. The hotel's blond and wicker furniture was sold after the hotel was closed in December of 1980. Following a fire in the hotel, plans to renovate the building failed. In 1998, the six-floor structure was demolished floor by floor with a wrecking ball. (Courtesy Dr. E. Russ Williams.)

HOTEL ALVIS LUXURY. This bed was part of the hotel's blond furniture sold after its closing in 1980. Note the monogrammed bedspread with "Hotel Alvis." (Courtesy Dr. E. Russ Williams.)

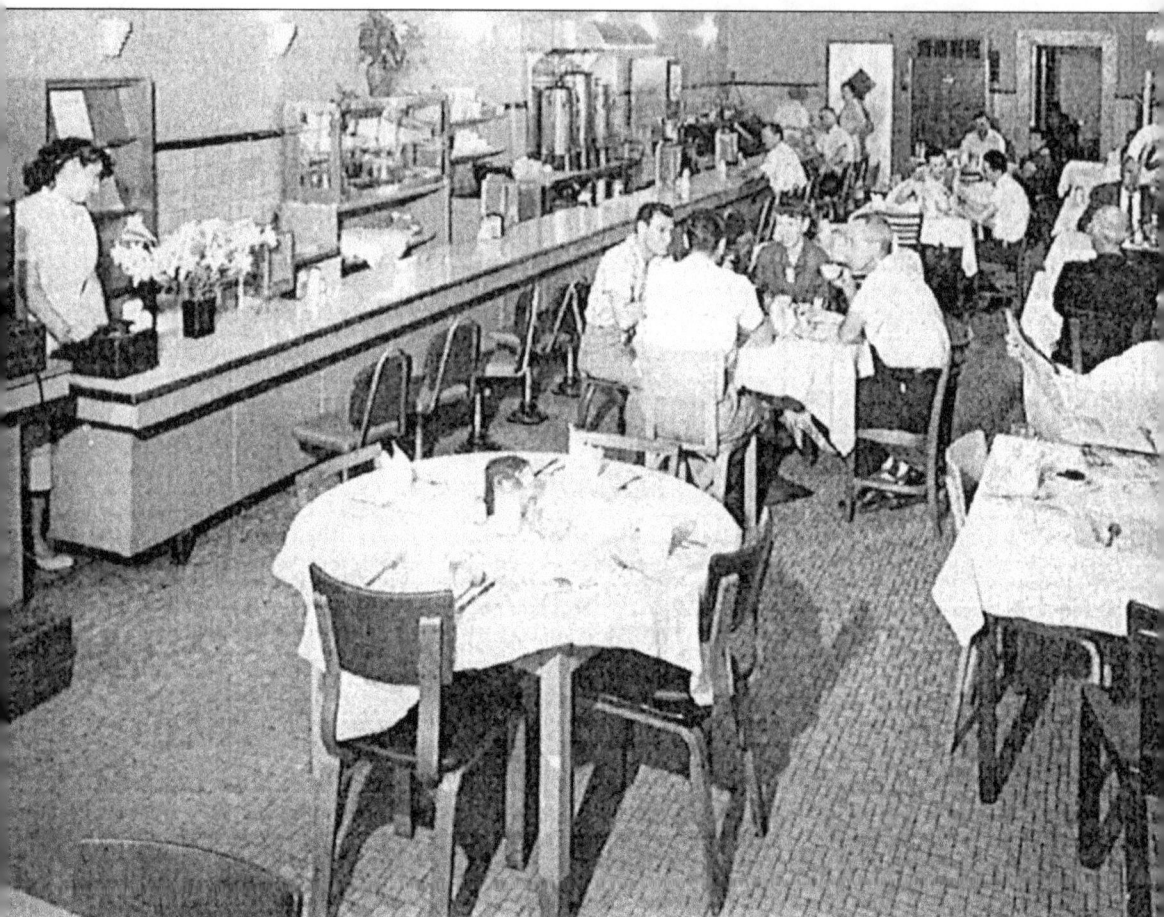

ALVIS HOTEL COFFEE SHOP. At one time, the Alvis had the finest coffee shop in northern Louisiana. People reputedly drove all the way from Shreveport, Louisiana, to eat there. (Courtesy Dr. E. Russ Williams.).

Five

FUN AND GAMES

SALTWATER NATATORIUM. Founded in 1910, the natatorium was located on Riverside Drive across from Forsythe Park. The pool was built during the administration of Mayor Andrew A. Forsythe. (Courtesy Ouachita Parish Public Library Special Collections Archives.)

SALT WATER NATATORIUM. C. 1920S. Where are the women swimmers? (Courtesy Ouachita Parish Public Library Special Collections Archives.)

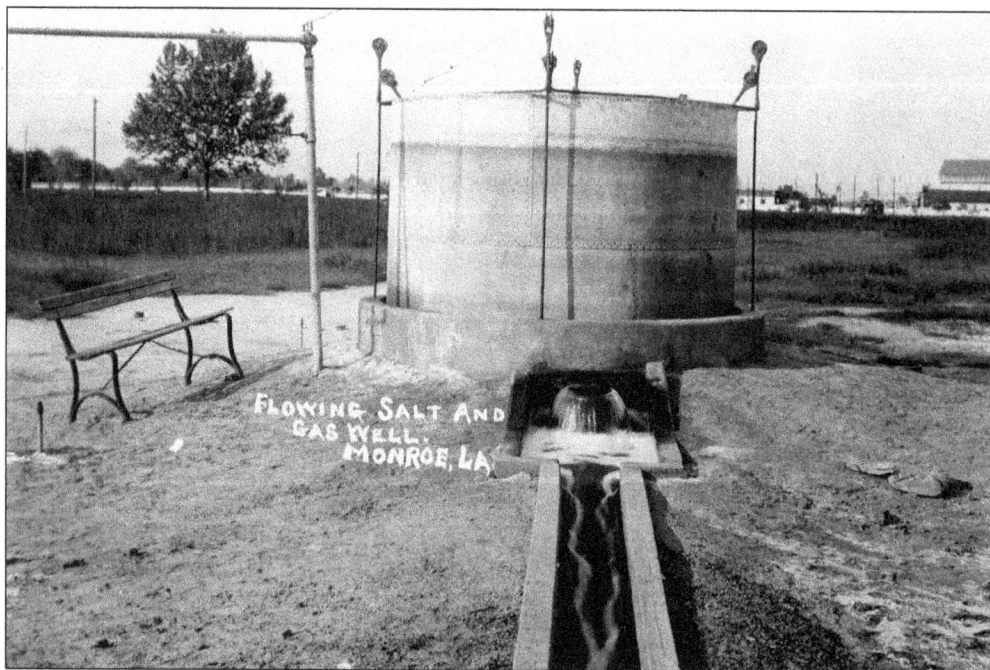

NATATORIUM. The old Natatorium was made possible by an accidental discovery. Drilling for gas in 1903 in Forsyth Park, Louis Lock hit a gusher of salt water. Finished in 1905 the pool was fed by the strong flow of high-density salt water from the well through an underground waterline, which ran under the site of Riverside Drive. After stagnation (despite chlorination) ruined the old pool, a new pool was built and finished in 1938. (Courtesy Ouachita Parish Public Library Special Collections Archives.)

PROGRESSIVE MEN'S CLUB. In 1927, the National Federation of Men's Clubs had their 28th annual convention on September 2–4, 1967, in Monroe. The city's Italian residents organized the club in 1931. The Progressive Men's Club was described as an active chapter of the National Federation of Young Men's Clubs and one of the outstanding organizations in the city of Monroe. The Monroe Chapter was one of the chapters instrumental in organizing the federation in 1932. The purposes and aims of the Progressive Men's Clubs are social, educational, and fraternal. Its formation came about through the efforts of several of the present leaders. Much has been accomplished in the years of its operation toward the realization of its aims. The Columbus Social Club of Monroe was also an Italian social club, comprised of the leading Italians of Monroe, holding as its duties to promote the general welfare and Americanization of Italians. The club is still in existence and meets in this building at 645 Highway 80 East. (Courtesy Sal Serio, New Orleans, Louisiana.)

BATHING BEAUTIES. A bevy of beautiful Twin City bathing beauties was photographed while they were posed at the Old Saltwater Natatorium in Monroe. Their dress was considered risqué attire *c.* 1919. Two women are identified as Bessie Reynolds and Victoria Schuster. (Courtesy Ouachita Parish Public Library Special Collections Archives.)

BESSIE REYNOLDS. Reynolds was a freshman at Ouachita Parish High School and is pictured in this 1915 freshman class photo. We couldn't match her with one of the bathing beauties above. Can you? (Courtesy Ouachita Parish Public Library Special Collections Archives.)

AN OUTING FOR THE LOUISIANA LAUNDRY OWNERS CLUB. Mr. Ahdfeld and Capt. G.B. Cooley are identified. The boats are identified as the *Weto* and *Weto Jr.* (Courtesy Dr. E. Russ Williams.)

AMERICAN LEGION HALL ON FORSYTHE AVENUE. It was decided in October 1927 that Leonidas Barkdale Faulk, Post No. 13, would build a hall. The City of Monroe donated the site on Forsythe Avenue and J.W. Smith & Associates, a Monroe architectural firm, designed the building. Only four years later, on January 6, 1931, "Unalaska," the leader of Admiral Byrd's dog team on his first Antarctic expedition, was buried on the grounds of the hall after having been killed by a hit-and-run driver in Monroe. (Courtesy Dr. E. Russ Williams.)

WOMEN'S VOLLEYBALL TEAM, OUACHITA PARISH HIGH SCHOOL 1931. According to *The Roarer*, "The girl's volleyball team, coached by Mr. Jack Hayes, went through their schedule this year with only one defeat to win the championship of North Louisiana for the fourth consecutive time. Mr. Hayes, perhaps, has the most remarkable record of any coach in the state. For eight consecutive years, he has produced champions." (Courtesy Ouachita Parish Public Library Special Collections Archives.)

OPHS TRACK TEAM. The 1930 OPHS track team was coached by Alf Reid. Gilbert Faulk, McMath Givens, Elston Swayze, David Pace, and Ernest Hinton are shown in the top photo. The track team members are not identified, but in 1930 they won fourth place at North Louisiana Track Meet and hoped for a better season the following year. (Courtesy Ouachita Parish Public Library Special Collections Archives.)

EARLY FOOTBALL TEAM AT OUACHITA PARISH HIGH. In the past, there was only one football team for Monroe schools. The mascot for those teams was a tiger. (Courtesy Ouachita Parish Public Library Special Collections Archives.)

OUACHITA PARISH HIGH SCHOOL BASKETBALL TEAM. Though the team members remain unidentified, they probably played between 1915 and 1920. (Courtesy Ouachita Parish Public Library Special Collections Archives.)

E.J. "BUNNY" SEVIERS. "Bunny" Seviers was a versatile Ouachita Parish High School halfback who starred as a member of the Lions' North Louisiana Class AA championship team in 1948. In 1949, he won the Lockhart-Blair sportsmanship trophy for his 1948 football season in Monroe. By 1952, he was playing defense for Northeast Louisiana State College. (Courtesy Ouachita Parish Public Library Special Collections Archives.)

OUACHITA PARISH HIGH SCHOOL FOOTBALL TEAM, 1932. There was much speculation about the age of the player on the ground to the right. The coaches, not pictured, were Ben Rush and George Riser. The players were (in no particular order) Brooks Owen (left half back), Pete Rasbury (right half back), Harry Stron (full back), Nelson Bland (quarterback), Sam Ebert (right end), Truman Staples (right tackle), John Frantom (right guard), David Pace (center), Mule Hooks (left guard), Kermit Youngblood (left tackle), Monroe Trimble (left end), Kent Breard (tackle), Clyde French (guard), Lynn McGuffy (half back), and Clifford Johnson (center). The team's record for the season was as follows: OPHS 19, Sarepta 6; OPHS 19, Lisbon, 6; OPHS 15, McGehee, Arkansas 13; OPHS 19, Delhi 0; OPHS 0, Haynesville 44; OPHS 25, Bastrop 6; OPHS 19, Ruston 0; OPHS 6, Bolton 0. (Courtesy Ouachita Parish Public Library Special Collections Archives.)

OUACHITA PARISH HIGH SCHOOL FOOTBALL TEAM, 1930. According to the 1931 *Roarer* yearbook, "The Lions established a better record this year than they had in years. The Jungle Kings won 7 games, tied 1 and lost 1 in the play-off for State Championship." Players included Bunny Kennedy, Pete Rasbury, Roland Brown, Tenille McEnery, Shelby Calhoun, Ivy McDonald, Durnell Witt, MacMath Giverns, Raymond Masling, Bill Bickhan, and Tom Pete Goodwin. (Courtesy Ouachita Parish Public Library Special Collections Archives.)

BREAKING GROUND AT BERNSTEIN PARK, 1952. A baseball field separate from the adult's was created for little league teams in Monroe. Given the date, the little league field was just beginning. Saul Adler was a very big promoter of baseball in the city. (Courtesy Temple B'Nai Israel Archives.)

ATHLETIC BASEBALL CLUB. The Monroe City League of 1912 is pictured above. The team members were only identified by their last names. In the center is Manager Mangham. Moving clockwise from the top center are Ammer, catcher; Williamson, center field; Gueriero, first base; Brooks, pitcher; Faulk, short stop and pitcher; Bynum, inner field; Wise, Newhall, out field; Marx, out field; Curl, second base; and Wolf. Player John J. Kelley's daughter-in-law contributed this photograph. The back of the picture gives the following information about Kelley: Athletics, 1912, field; Cubs, 1911, pitcher; Old Grand Dads, 1913, field; Federals, 1914, catcher. Kelley's batting average is listed as .315. Kelley, who died in 1960, was executive vice president of Monroe Automobile and Supply Company. (Courtesy Ouachita Parish Public Library Special Collections Archives.)

DAVE CHEEVERS. Dave Cheevers played professional baseball briefly for Monroe. The Monroe professional baseball teams had the following names during Dave's playing years: the Drillers 1924–1932; the Cotton States League; and the Twins 1937. (Courtesy Don Linebarger.)

Negro World Series 1932

The Monroe Monarchs won the 1932 pennant in the Southern League. They played the winners of the pennant in the National League, the Pittsburg Crawfords, in the 1932 Negro World Series.

MONROE MONARCHS, NEGRO WORLD SERIES, 1932. Robert Peterson author of *Only the Ball was White*, a book about the team, wrote the following:

> In spite of segregation, The Monarchs of Monroe, Louisiana, lived fairly well due to the beneficence of the owner of the team, white drilling-company operator J.C. Stovall. He built a fine ballpark with an adjoining swimming pool and dance pavilion for Monroe's Negroes because he felt that since he made his living in part from the city's black population, it was only right that he offer them free recreation. Stovall also built a strong club, and the Monarchs were Negro baseball powers in the late 1920s and early 1930s. Their stadium was equal to most good minor-league fields of that time. After the Negro Club was disbanded, the park was leased to the white Monroe team in the Old Cotton States League, a class-D circuit.

(Courtesy Ouachita Parish Public Library Special Collections Archives.)

onroe Sports 1950"

n Willis - Bobby Johnson - Jim Burns - Allen Cross - Roy Coss - Virgil Bivins - Turkey Lurk - Cliff Coggin
Paul Mannasch, Mgr......
a Morrison - Jim Pace - Bill Tremel - Wayne Moon - Al Mazur - Carl Tucker - Charlie Cline - Bill Moffet
Photo by Earl B. Williams.

MONROE SPORTS, 1950. This team probably played in the Ball Park Building for which funds were being collected in 1949. The American Legion in Monroe headed the public campaign to provide Monroe and West Monroe with a modern baseball park. By February 23, 1949, $23,781 had been donated. An agreement had been reached with the Shreveport Club of the Texas League to provide Monroe with a baseball team. If a berth in the Cotton States League could not be obtained, Shreveport was to supply a semi-professional club for Monroe for the 1949 season. (Courtesy Temple B'Nai Israel Archives.)

COTTON STATES LEAGUE CHAMPIONS. Dr. W.L. Bendel is pictured on the far right. (Courtesy Temple B'Nai Israel Archives.)

ELKS LODGE, NO. 454. This wagon was part of the Elks Lodge's exhibit in the Flower Parade that took place on October 21, 1910, at the Monroe State Fair. (Courtesy Dr. E. Russ Williams.)

OVERS LANE, MONROE, LA.

100558

LOVER'S LANE. Pictured above is the view of Lover's Lane looking south from the intersection of South Grand and Carolina Streets. Originally called South Grand Street, Lover's Lane became a favorite rendezvous spot for young couples. The Catalpa trees lining the street were once fence posts planted by Hypolite Pargoud in the early 1800s; the trees are still growing today. (Courtesy Ouachita Parish Public Library Special Collections Archives.)

LOVELY LADIES. These ladies are shown on Lover's Lane, c. late 1800s. (Courtesy Ouachita Parish Public Library Special Collections Archives.)

GLOOM CHASERS BAND AND FLYER. Bernhardt's Gloom Chasers were a popular dance orchestra in the 1920s in Monroe. Phillip Bernhardt of Monroe owned the orchestra from 1920 to 1925. In 1929, Bernhardt organized Bernhardt Music Company. (Courtesy Dr. E. Russ Williams.)

Back Again   Eight Pieces

BERNHARDT'S
GLOOM CHASERS

The Boys Who Made The Fourth of July Famous

TO PLAY FOR
NATCHEZ' NEATEST AND NICEST

DANCE

UNDER SUPERVISION OF YOUNG GENTLEMEN

FRIDAY, JULY 25, 1924
MEMORIAL HALL

Dancing: Nine 'till--"It Ain't Gonna Rain No More"

YOUR FRIENDS ARE INVITED

GENTLEMEN with TWO LADIES, TWO DOLLARS
LADIES WITHOUT ESCORT, FIFTY CENTS

GLOOM CHASERS. Although newspapers of the time undoubtedly carried announcements of the gigs the Gloom Chasers played, little is known about the band and its members. (Courtesy Dr. E. Russ Williams.)

93

OUACHITA FAIR. In September 1986, the Ouachita Parish Fair was held in Monroe. (Courtesy Ouachita Parish Public Library Special Collections Archives.)

ANNUAL AFFAIR. The Fall Parish Fair is an annual event at the Monroe Civic Center, a small portion of which can be seen in the far left of this photo. (Courtesy Ouachita Parish Public Library Special Collections Archives.)

MONROE GRAMMAR SCHOOL BAND. Picture taking was part of the duties of the Louisiana Writers' Project. The picture here is that of a band performance on St. John Street in the mid-1930s in front of the First Baptist Church of Monroe. (Courtesy Ouachita Parish Public Library Special Collections Archives.)

GLOOM CHASERS. (Courtesy Dr. E. Russ Williams.)

GLOOM CHASERS. (Courtesy Dr. E. Russ Williams.)

Six

LOCAL BUSINESSES

FERD LEVI BUILDING. J.B. Block Wholesale Liquors was located on the ground floor of the Ferd Levi Building. (Courtesy Temple B'Nai Israel Archives.)

DELIVERY TRUCKS. This delivery door could not be definitely identified, but the photo was probably taken during the late 1920s. Business must have been good, judging from the number of delivery trucks. (Courtesy Temple B'Nai Israel Archives.)

CENTRAL SAVINGS BANK AND TRUST, SOUTH GRAND STREET. The charter for the bank was approved in 1905 and its doors opened in 1906. In the middle of the Depression, Delta Air Lines was organized in the bank's boardroom. In 1962, the boardroom was dedicated as "The Delta Room." In 1919, Central offered 3.5 percent on savings accounts. The clock was added in 1926. Also shown in the photo is Griffin Studios, an elite photography studio in Monroe until the early 1980s. (Courtesy Ouachita Parish Public Library Special Collections Archives.)

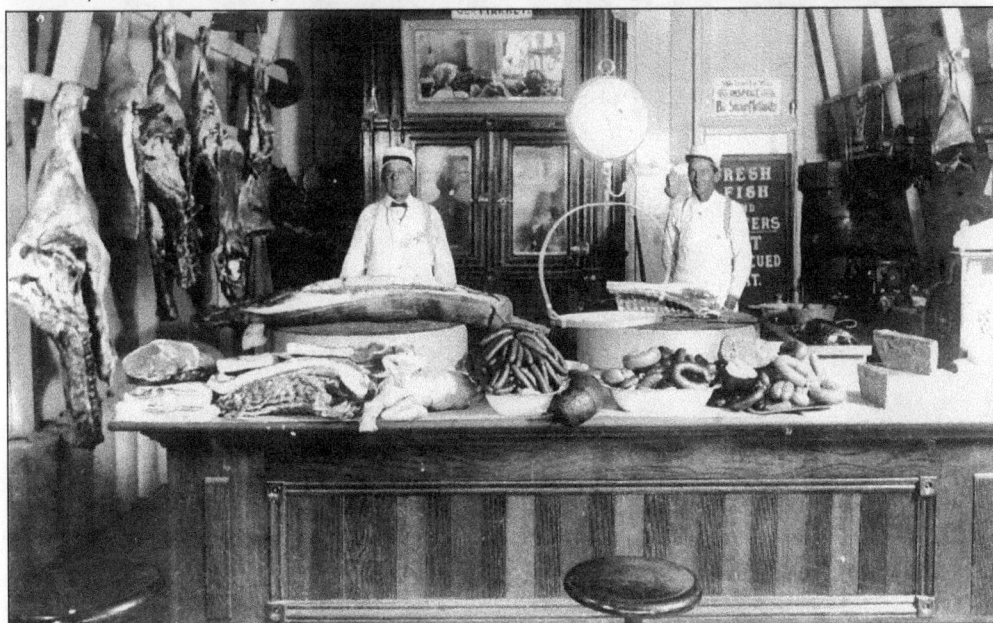

FAULK BROTHERS GROCERY AND FEED STUFFS. The store was located at 518 South Grand Street, Monroe, Louisiana. Will Faulk is seen on the right. (Courtesy Ouachita Parish Public Library Special Collections Archives.)

FAULK BROTHERS GROCERIES AND FEEDSTUFFS. This grocery store was located at 518 South Grand Street. Note Isaiah Garrett's house on the left. (Courtesy Ouachita Parish Public Library Special Collections Archives.)

FAULK BROTHERS GROCERY. This grocery was located 518 South Grand. (Courtesy Ouachita Parish Public Library Special Collections Archives.)

MILK WAGON. This delivery wagon carried milk from the dairy to Roland Road and was then picked up by a larger milk transporter. (Courtesy Dr. E. Russ Williams.)

MONROE STEAM LAUNDRY. The banner advertised the laundry's Visitors Week and proclaimed that, "We invite you to see our modern up to date plant in operation. Come October 23 to 28." (Courtesy Ouachita Parish Public Library Special Collections Archives.)

MONROE STEAM LAUNDRY, 1905. The laundry wanted customers to know that they were "Improving [their] equipment, bettering [their] service." (Courtesy Ouachita Parish Public Library Special Collections Archives.)

MONROE STEAM LAUNDRY READY TO ROLL. The laundry served many Monroe customers and therefore needed this large fleet of delivery trucks. The laundry was begun in 1895 by G.B. Cooley. It began with eight employees. The laundry was located at 436–442 South Grand. (Courtesy Ouachita Parish Public Library Special Collections Archives.)

MONROE STEAM LAUNDRY. Note the uniformed delivery men. In 1905 Mr. Cooley gave employment to a force of over 30 people and operated a line of wagons that covered the entire city and suburbs of Monroe. Cooley also operated an extensive out-of-town shipping trade

through agents. The company made a specialty of the Shirt, Collar, and Cuff Department. (Courtesy Ouachita Parish Public Library Special Collections Archives.)

LEON MARX CAFÉ. The lady in the center of the photo is Leon's sister, Rose Lee Marx. (Courtesy Dr. E. Russ Williams.)

Monroe Hardware Co., Ltd.

HEAVY AND SHELF HARDWARE

Agricultural Implements, Mill Supplies, Wagons, Buggies, Harness, Stoves and Ranges

DISTRIBUTORS OF THE

Feather Edge Brand of Fine Cutlery, Files and Edged Tools of Every Description.

MONROE, LOUISIANA

Shell Hardware Department.
Interior of Office.

Heavy Hardware Department.
Warehouse.

MONROE HARDWARE CO., LTD. Founded in 1878 by Sublett Brothers, the store became Monroe Hardware Company, Ltd in 1889. Aside from the usual shelf hardware, wagons, buggies, agricultural implements, they specialized in fine cutlery and edged tools of every description. They also sold Studebaker wagons and carriages. It was located at 117–123 St. John. (Courtesy Ouachita Parish Public Library Special Collections Archives.)

STANDARD ESSO STATION. The station is located on the corner of South Grand and Grammont Streets; it occupies the space that was once Saul Adler's Garage in the late 1930s to 1940s. The Penn Hotel is in the background. (Courtesy Temple B'Nai Israel Archives.)

BREARD MERCANTILE STORE. The store was located at Desiard and Grand Streets in Monroe. The original of this photograph was made c. 1885. The photographer is unknown. (Courtesy of Ouachita Parish Public Library Special Collections Archives, donated by John Vaughan, Monroe, Louisiana.)

Sig Haas & Sons. Sig Haas, senior member of the firm Sig Haas & Sons, was born in Bavaria, Germany, June 29, 1856. He obtained his early education in Germany. At 16, he came to the United States and garnered a position as a clerk in a store in Grand Lake, Arkansas. He later moved to Fort Worth, Texas, and from there, to Monroe. He worked for Meyer Brothers Merchandise Co. until 1900 when he founded the Famous Company. In 1906, he sold his interest in the Famous Company and started his own business. He was a member of the Western

Star Lodge No. 24 F&A.M of which he was a master for five years. He was an exalted ruler of the Elks Lodge, a member of B'Nai Birth, director of the Ouachita National Bank, and one of the organizers of the Monroe Building and Loan Association. He was also a president of the Louisiana League, Homestead, and the Building and Loan Association. He married Miss Dora Behrman of Monroe in 1882 and had two sons. (Courtesy Temple B'Nai Israel Archives.)

SUGAR THEATRE BUILDING, 301-305 DESIARD STREET. The Sugar Brothers owned a number of business firms in 1912. They constructed two theatre buildings in Monroe. Notice that the upstairs corner of the building says "Vaudeville Moving Pictures." (Courtesy Temple B'Nai Israel Archives.)

AUSTIN'S RESTAURANT. This site was formerly the site of the old Western Union Station at the corner of Desiard and South Grand. (Courtesy Ouachita Parish Public Library Special Collections Archives.)

BAYLES' FISH MARKET. Now Gabbeaux' Bayles Landing, the restaurant has been a popular one in West Monroe for many years. It is located on the Ouachita River at the foot of the Endom Bridge. (Courtesy Ouachita Parish Public Library Special Collections Archives.)

ILLINOIS CENTRAL RAILROAD STATION, 1980. These photographs are particularly significant because the railroad station burned March 6, 2002. (Courtesy Ouachita Parish Public Library Special Collections.)

Seven

FLOODS

AUSTIN AVENUE, WEST MONROE, 1932. Before the flood waters receded they had reached even higher stages than what is pictured here. (Courtesy Ouachita Parish Public Library Special Collections Archives.)

BROWN PAPER MILL DURING THE 1932 FLOOD. H. Luther Brown established the vast Brown Paper Mill in West Monroe before 1927, so the facility was flooded not only in 1932, but in 1927 as well. (Courtesy Ouachita Parish Public Library Special Collections Archives.)

CROSLEY SCHOOL DURING THE 1932 FLOOD. Located still at 700 Natchitoches Street in West Monroe, Crosley Elementary School was built in 1916. (Courtesy Ouachita Parish Public Library Special Collections Archives.)

114

DAM ACROSS THE LITTLE BLACK, WEST MONROE, 1932. Dams such as this were common in flood times. Note the armed guard. (Courtesy Ouachita Parish Public Library Special Collections Archives.)

ELMER SLAGLE RESIDENCE AT 1600 SOUTH GRAND. This photo was taken by Griffin in the 1932 flood. Elmer Slagle was the Secretary General of Slagle Johnson Lumber Company in the early 1900s. (Courtesy Ouachita Parish Public Library Special Collections Archives.)

GRIFFIN RESIDENCE DURING 1932 FLOOD. This is the intersection of South Grand and Pear Streets in Monroe. The photographer who captured these images died in 1932. He caught a cold that turned into pneumonia while trying to protect his family's house, pictured in this photo. He had opened the business in 1915. His son, Durwood Griffin, continued to operate the business until 1983. (Courtesy Ouachita Parish Public Library Special Collections Archives.)

HOLMES RESIDENCE DURING FLOOD OF 1927. The residents of this home were probably the family of George S. Holmes, first vice-president and general manager of The Brown Paper Mill in West Monroe. (Courtesy Ouachita Parish Public Library Special Collections Archives.)

LOUISIANA TRAINING INSTITUTE IN THE FLOOD OF 1932. Louisiana Training Institute is located on South Grand Street in Monroe. No area of the city was exempt from the damage. (Courtesy Ouachita Parish Public Library Special Collections Archives.)

MONROE FLOOD 1932. To the right of the picture is the "Old Windmill," a tourist attraction at the Old Saltwater Natatorium. It served no purpose and collapsed over time. Note that there was no levee when this photo was taken. (Courtesy Ouachita Parish Public Library Special Collections Archives.)

MONROE-RAYVILLE HIGHWAY, FLOOD OF 1927. Richland Parish (where Rayville is located) was flooded by backwaters from the tributaries of the Mississippi. This fact is important to note because Richland parish is far inland but was, nevertheless, heavily flooded. Residents built boats hoping that they would not have to use them. Unfortunately, they were required to do so. (Courtesy Ouachita Parish Public Library Special Collections Archives.)

OLD SALTWATER NATATORIUM DURING THE 1927 FLOOD. Ironically, it was this flood water that ruined the saltwater Natatorium. (Courtesy Ouachita Parish Public Library Special Collections Archives.)

NATATORIUM DURING FLOOD OF 1932. After the 1932 flood, the Natatorium shut down. It had never re-opened after the flood of 1927. (Courtesy of Ouachita Parish Public Library Special Collections Archives.)

ANOTHER VIEW OF A FLOOD REFUGEE CAMP, 1927. Most of the camps were located in West Monroe because it was on higher ground. National Guardsmen were needed here as well as along the levees. The Red Cross Camp was located at the McGuire Place (Traveler's Rest Plantation). (Courtesy Dr. E. Russ Williams.)

RIVERSIDE COUNTRY CLUB, FLOODED. The sign reads "Private Club." In flood times, however, everyone shared the same tragedies. Toughened laborers and tenderfeet worked side by side sand bagging and doing whatever was necessary. (Courtesy Ouachita Parish Public Library Special Collections Archives.)

WEST MONROE FLOOD 1932. The 1932 flood in Northeast Louisiana affected the Ouachita-Boeuf floodplain even more than the 1927 flood. (Courtesy Ouachita Parish Public Library Special Collections Archives.)

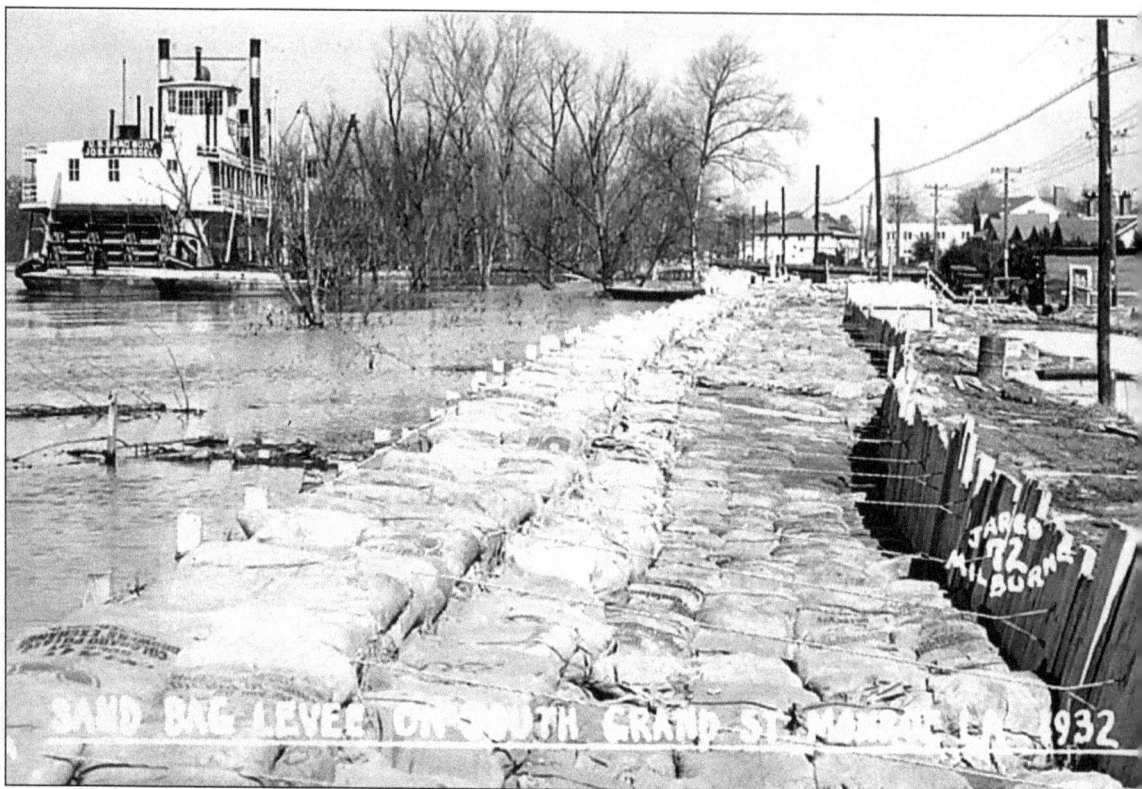

SAND BAG LEVEE. This sandbag levee is seen on South Grand Street during the 1932 flood. (Courtesy Ouachita Parish Public Library Special Collections Archives.)

FLOOD PICTURE, 1927. In the left bottom corner is Strauss Co., Inc., Wholesale Dry Goods. (Courtesy Ouachita Parish Public Library Special Collections Archives.)

WEST MONROE FLOOD 1932. The people in this photograph appear to be evacuating from their homes. The waters promised to continue rising. (Courtesy Ouachita Parish Public Library

WEST MONROE, LA
2-6-32

Special Collections Archives.)

Visit us at
arcadiapublishing.com

www.ingramcontent.com/pod-product-compliance
Lightning Source LLC
Chambersburg PA
CBHW050701110426
42813CB00007B/2052